wild spirit, soft heart

- butterflies rising -

ISBN: 978-0-578-64354-0 (Paperback)

butterfliesrising.com
butterfliesrisingpoetry.com
gowhereyoubreathefree.com
go where you breathe free™
shesflowersandfire.com

poetry, quotes, thoughts, feelings…

little pieces of my soul

wild spirit, soft heart

This book title comes from a quote I put out a few years ago, "wild spirit, soft heart, sweet soul," which is a shortened version of another quote of mine, and before I even truly knew whether or not I was capable of writing this book, I knew this title was meant to be if I ever could. It all comes from a dynamic of wild and soft within me, and within my life. It's this combination of fierce independence and a strong need for my own individual soul's journey that I have, but also a magnetic pull to the energy of love and soulmates and connection that I have always felt. It has been the most powerful dynamic in my soul's journey on so many levels. It's been part of my journey in really beautiful and magical ways, and in heartbreaking and complicated ways, too. So, when you read this book, you'll see the energies of wild and soft, of passion and tenderness, and of self-love and soulmate love running through it all; along with the energy of what it is to be a soft and sensitive soul who has gone through hard things. It all has to do with the many layers that I hold within myself, and with the soft and hard parts of my journey, and also to do with a deep connection I have to the dance between feminine and masculine energies. The combination of flowers and fire is so much a part of who I am and the things I've been through, that it just spills out into my writing. These words truly are pieces of my soul. So, I hope that when you read this book that my heart and soul come through. And I also hope that maybe my words speak to your heart and soul in some way, too.

self-love

wild spirit, soft heart, sweet soul

just a girl growing wings

the first step in

setting yourself free...

i am willing to grow.

....

This is my agreement with myself. In all of the places and circumstances and situations in my life where I feel stuck, to be willing to grow. To be willing to listen to what something is showing to me or asking from me. To understand that even though I may not have control over things happening around me, or even always to me, I am still always responsible for my own energy within those experiences. And I can still always look for movement and change within my own space that I hold. And that's where my freedom will come from. So, instead of fighting against the things outside of me that may make me feel like I'm stuck, being open to where I can grow, *to grow out of them.*

this becoming
will ask for your breath, patience
and for your fight, perseverance

transformation is made of both
surrender and strength

this is a growing season,
of change, of turning, of shedding,
of letting things fall away, and fall apart,
and come undone, and be uncovered

and then a space of surrender, and being, *just being.*

and the reflections here are temporary,
so take them in and honor them,
and be honest with them, and own them...
but then forgive them, and don't stay in them

let it all go... let yourself bloom

in a wilderness,
with an unheld hand,
you will learn
to love yourself just as madly,
with the fierceness,
the recklessness,
that you have loved them

self-love...

the most delicate intimacy

i'm still learning
how to hear the word *beautiful*
and let it be meant for me

...to breathe it in
and let it belong here

i have to learn

to feel good

in my own

before it

can feel good

to be next

to someone else's

- skin

i'm still learning how to be mine

mine

it often takes
for someone to invite us to feel it,
but never return it,
and to deprive us of it where it should've been,
to cause us to ache for it enough
when it's nowhere else to be found,
for us to finally seek it within

- *the love*

we carry all the weight,
and we create all the beauty,
until we learn that we deserve someone
who carries their own weight,
and radiates their own beauty

- *the evolution of worth*

you have a
beautiful heart, babygirl,
and it's meant to know
a beautiful love

you are more than
enough to hold someone's
full attention,

don't settle for anyone who
tries to come to you with
theirs divided.

you've been chasing down
the kind of love
that greets you with nothing more
than a shoulder shrug...
the kind that whimpers your name in apathy,

don't you know that you deserve a love
that holds so much abundance,
one that shouts to the heavens in your honor

queen/king

the universe
burst stars open
and let the pieces fall
and they settled into a shape
and it was given your name
and your heart was placed inside
with all your magic buried in it
with moondust on the edges
and all your flowers planted with it
and this is you...
this is all inside of you.
so how could anyone
ever look at you
and not be breathtakingly fascinated
by the wonder of it all

settling will always
leave the heart
relentlessly unsettled

if anyone or anything
needs my spirit to be small...

i'm finally learning
to walk away

Sun-flavored Love...

i've learned that
i deserve more than a starved love...
that kind where you feed off of me
because you can't fill yourself

i deserve rich love, extra love
abundant and sun-flavored and overflowing on me
because you're full within yourself

my power has been,
in spite of *everything*, always
finding it in me somewhere
to say to myself... *you are worthy.*

vibrate so high,
and radiate from so deep,
from so much within your heart,
from your essence, from your soul,
so that no one can come close to you
without destiny's blessing
in their hands

and every time they
try to make you feel unworthy...

just go towards yourself.
choose to love yourself more.
and build such an unshakable bond with
your worth that there's just nothing they
can ever do to take you away from it.

i hope you know...
you matter now.
chosen by no one.
belonging to yourself.

Poetry Heart...

do you really believe
that you were given this poetry heart,
and filled up with all this magic you hold,
and made capable of such big love,
to have it all be meant for someone
who treated you that way...

they were not the one.

i have worried my heart
far too much about what i am worth
to those who were not worthy
of my heart

what is
beautiful in me
and what is tender
in me

it is always.

no matter how
hard you tried to make
me feel hard to love

there are
all these beautiful
and tender things in me…
always.

save
yourself
for people who
always treat you
in such a way
that lets you love
yourself

in such a way

love won't ask you to be
less of yourself,
it will invite you to become more
and more of you,
to step into all of you

this love
comes sweetly
this gentle awakening
like warmth on your skin
and a breath on your neck
let it say so softly...

you are more than enough.

and there is
too much good in you
for you to not let goodness
be who and what you are

if you can't help
but love with raw vulnerability,
just let it be a beautiful way about you,
some things are going to hurt like a force,
but the beautiful things will be *magic.*

learn to let
yourself feel the soft things
when they come to you

these soft, quiet,
intimate moments
that your heart is beating
are precious,
so if it takes
you out of your peace,
don't give it your
little moments

i am safe.
i am worthy.
i am loved.

if i am to
feel sure of anything,
i must learn to feel
sure of me

i'm learning
to love the way
my name settles
in silence
before i can love
how it falls
from another's
mouth

- *this love story first.*

sweet girl,
it wasn't that you weren't enough,
it's your energy... it asks
others to rise up, and not everyone
is willing to go where they
would grow

your heart is too
special to not be carried
kindly, to not be held like
it's magic

too special

on your own
is where your
wildflowers grow,
there's no one else here to
block their sun,
but no one else can water
them but you

there is this
stunning breathing rhythm
in a woman learning to love herself

this slow rise as she feels her way into
every inch of her skin like honey,
and this soft fall as she settles into grace

this is the breath i seek

honey and grace

i've learned to
be gentle with that part of
me that takes it in so deeply
and holds on to it for far too long,

that's also the part of me that loves
like an awakening and knows what it's like
to trace a soul in my fingertips

....

It wasn't until I was 19 that I learned what an empath is. But when I did it was also when I first started understanding myself.

I was raised pretty sheltered philosophically, mostly Southern Baptist, and so as far as spirituality went, I was only really exposed to traditional religious beliefs. If it wasn't in the Bible, or if the preacher didn't teach it, it just wasn't part of the spiritual speak in my world. "Empath" wasn't a word I ever heard. All of my sensitivity and intuition didn't have an explanation... and I just really didn't know what to do with any of it.

But when I was 17 I left home, and I left the church at the same time. Not because I was running from spirituality, but because I was desperately craving it. I don't fault anyone who truly finds their peace or guidance within the church or organized religion, but I had just never found what I was searching for there. And I was *aching* for it. So, I kind of went full abandon into every direction of any kind of spiritual teachings that I could find.

One of the places that my searches led me to was a yoga studio in Nashville where my teacher was this magnetic French woman who was full of stories and lessons and knowledge, and I gravitated to her like a baby Jedi wanting to take in every bit of The Force that she could teach me. She was so open and loving and free spirited, and the things she spoke about and the books she guided me to... it was the kind of soul food I had been craving. So, she was the person who explained to me what an empath is. And when she did, finally everything about why I have always felt the way I feel in this world started to make sense.

Understanding that all of this excruciating sensitivity in me is how I am "made," that it's *on purpose*, has been one of the most freeing gifts I've ever been given. I know now that *feeling. so. much.* is just part of who I am, and that it gives life to the things about me that are beautiful. It gives me kindness and empathy and softness, it feeds my creativity and curiosity and adventurous spirit, and it gives a pulse to the way I live and love and experience everything in this life. I feel it all so deeply, and I take so much of it in, but that makes this life vibrant and powerful. It *all* affects my soul... and I think having my soul be affected is *why I'm here*, and it's how I grow.

It's also been powerful for navigating how overwhelming it can be. It's given me an understanding that all of this constant intake of energy means that not everything I feel or take in and take on, is mine. And having an awareness of that has helped me so much in putting it down or letting it go when it isn't mine.

So, I've learned to be gentle with it. It's why it can all hurt so much, but it's why things can be so incredibly beautiful, too.

let the
wonder and beauty
of your existence
fall out of you
everywhere, unafraid
no matter who may take it in
or hold it with care
let it all be
unshaken by the cold

the wonder
and beauty of your existence

feel
everything
that is
beautiful and possible
in your soul,
and let yourself
become it

let yourself be
a many-layered thing

you are allowed to be lovely
and important,
to speak up, and out, and convicted
from the same mouth that tends
to love and cradles lilies

it's stunning when you let
why you're here spill out of you

beautiful wildflower, grow untamed

let a new version of you
be uncovered

healing

healing is an intimate,
delicate,
unique,
fingerprint...

take the journey you need
to get there

be gentle with
the way you're learning to
hold your own heart

....

If there's anything I've learned about healing, it's that it isn't linear. It's layered and messy and it asks us to have so, *so* much compassion with ourselves. My own healing process has been taking me through every extreme of growth and unlearning and learning... from the depths of victimhood and codependency, to the darkest places of shame and self-doubt. And it's a constant search for my truth somewhere in between all of the extremes. A balance between healing from the hurt that others have caused me, but then also taking full responsibility for my own energy and choices and faults and mistakes... but again, having compassion with all of it, and learning to hold myself on my own.

this is going
to feel different someday,
it will lose its hold on your
breath... *even this.*

heartbreak has this way
of making your world seem so small,
just taking everything that
has meaning and collapsing it into
one single story, with only one other person,
and just one version of yourself, in just
one version of life, with what feels
like no way out, and as if there is
nothing more to know

but this world is too wide, and this
universe is too big, and you are *just. too. beautiful,*
and there is just way too much inside of you...
for you to let this be the end

this isn't the end...

....

Whenever I've been really, *really* heartbroken in my life, there's this thing that has happened in the deepest parts of the heartbreak... this thing where my world has felt incredibly small. And I think that's a very *human* thing. When we love someone deeply or care about something intensely, our identity, our reality, our world... they're all shaped with the notion that the people we love, and the things we care about, are all part of those things. And so, when a connection or a situation in our life just *ends*, it can feel as if the world we know has crashed in.

When my first love broke my heart, my world crashed in. He hadn't been just a boyfriend, he had been a protector and a sort of "spiritual guidance" in my life. So, the loss of that connection left me feeling lost in who I was, and I went *excruciatingly* internal with my healing process. And because of how deep I went with it, I was struggling to move the pain out of me. And one night during that time it all built up inside of me and I just had to get out of my head and go *somewhere.* So, I packed up enough for a road trip, and having no clue where I was going, I just got in my car and drove.

I drove west out of Nashville until Nashville became Memphis, and then Memphis became Arkansas, and then Arkansas became a road trip. And in the following days, I wandered through Texas, and through New Mexico, and I stood by myself on the edge of the Grand Canyon, and I almost ran out of gas in Death Valley, and I watched the sunset over Mono Lake... and finally, about 2 weeks later, I reached the end of my trip watching the sunrise in Lake Tahoe.

And while I was standing on the Tahoe shoreline, I knew that I wasn't quite the same girl who had left Nashville 2 weeks before. Not that much had actually changed in my life, but my perspective had. I spent that trip seeing so many beautiful things, and reminding myself how wide the world was, and seeing how much life was still out there for me. And it helped me start to understand that what had just ended was only a chapter in my life closing, and that it wasn't the end of my entire story.

And I've had even more devastating heartbreak in my life since then, but I think that feeling I felt that morning in Tahoe has stayed with me through the other heartbreaks. It's given me a deep internal knowing that the things that shatter my world are not just cold, hard endings... they are transitions. And whenever my world is shattered, I'll eventually heal the broken pieces and start to create a new one.

they didn't take pieces of you,
don't give the people who hurt you that power

they broke loose, and dislodged,
and extracted pieces of you
that could just no longer stay part of you
and who you're becoming

so as you're letting those people go,
be willing to let those pieces go too

...let a new version of you
be uncovered

sometimes the universe will
remove or withhold, not to hurt you,
but to free you or save you from
what doesn't lead you home

what your heart
can't settle...
just give it to the universe

help me trust that
there's a beautiful purpose
in this broken heart

it's been torn,
and tattered,
and broken apart,
but keep me vulnerable
and broken open,
please stay
my tender heart

i've been held
by rough hands...
and i'm still healing.
to let a good man, be a good man,
it takes a new way...
and i'm still learning.

- *recovery*

i used to
think it was beautiful
the way i offered you all of my softness
and filled the air with tenderness
in the wake of your violence...
but now i know that i deserve to breathe
in tenderness too.

....

There's this thing that's not often talked about when it comes to the subject of "how a woman could put up with how she was treated," or *why* she stayed in a destructive relationship.

It's not always fear, or need, or even as simple as low self-worth. It's not always because we failed to run from harmful things that we were taught to run from. Sometimes it's because we embraced harmful things that we were taught to embrace. It's because we went *towards* what we were taught love looks like, and what a woman's role in love looks like. It's not only a "Southern" thing, but growing up in the South, and in a very religious and patriarchal family, I was raised with strong visuals of what I can only describe as "romanticized" ideals of a woman's role in unhealthy relationships.

"Stand by your man."

If he disrespects you, if he takes you for granted, if he cheats, if he drinks way too much, if he hits, if he rages, if he harms his children... the women I grew up around didn't leave. They stayed. They loved harder. And they softened the room. That was a woman's *"job." Love* meant that you'll put up with anything from him, and you'll do your best to fix him, fill him, heal him, and soften his hard ways. It's what a "good woman" does. And it's not just that she is judged if she doesn't play that role, it's that she is also *praised* when she does. Catering to a man's worst self was this normalized, expected, and even respected and glorified thing.

So, when I got into my second relationship, I fell into that role of "a soft woman saving a hard man" like I was coming on home. And when this 6'5" stereotype of masculinity with a raging unkindness inside of him was towering over 5'5" me in a little summer dress with my soft Southern accent, I thought it was *some kind of magic* the way I could calm him. The way I could break the violence he was building inside of him, and just wrap him up in sweet. I was some kind of angel the way I could settle his demons... *right?* I truly thought it was this "beautiful thing" that I had some type of way with his darkness.

It never occurred to me that I shouldn't have had to. It had just been so normalized to me that it was my job as a woman to *be so good* that a man *becomes good for me.* I didn't yet understand that a good man needs to be a good man from the inside out, and for himself, regardless of his proximity to a woman, or to anyone else. Both women and men deserve that.

In that relationship, he only ever got physical with me once. I don't describe it as *only once* to downplay it. I say it that way because I remember how in my skewed understanding, it felt like it was that "beautiful dynamic" of soft and hard that there was between us that "let it only happen once." And when I was growing up, the violence in my home was regularly physical, so that made "only once" seem like a safe place in comparison.

And it's also why I didn't see the harmful things that were happening in that relationship as abuse. His violence wasn't physical, so I didn't think it was violence. The mood swings, the lying, the manipulation, the controlling behavior, the triangulation, and all of the other little tiny ways of breaking me down and trying to make me unsure of myself... it was all sort of intangible. But still *so* violent. And the worst part was how he could be so, so beautiful to me. It was the worst part because, ultimately, it wasn't real. It was just a way to convince me that what was happening was "love." Just a way to make me feel safe before the next round of mood swings, and lying, and manipulation, and triangulation, and control. It was all just a way to keep me reaching for that "soft side of him that only I could so beautifully bring out from underneath his hardened shell."

It's been a slow process healing those unconscious behavior patterns in me, but I'm at least aware of them now, and I'm determined to continue healing them. I also understand now that it isn't my responsibility to fix, fill, or heal a man. And that I deserve to be with someone who takes responsibility for his own healing and his own self-love. And I will never again put up with or cater to a man's worst self, in any way. And now, when I look back at that relationship and remember those times that he was soft with me, and kind to me, and beautiful to me, whether or not it was real, I just remember that it felt really good. And the more I grow into myself, when I think about what love looks like now, I think of it as a place where someone will truly be soft, and kind, and beautiful to me.

i didn't know how to measure my worth,
and it led me to someone who measured his worth
in attention from her, and also *her*, and *her*...
and any other her to hurt me

he thought there was power in possession and pain,
and that a man's kingdom should be built
on the stepping of her back and the forfeit of her crown

so i forfeited. and i faded. but i'm learning things...

like how real lovers don't come in numbers. they aren't prisoners.
they're not meant to be suffocated, or left for granted...
and how i'm full enough of wonder to hold someone's attention,
that my full voice *matters*,
my full-bodied existence is beautiful,
and that a man on the strong side of oppression isn't
the same thing as a man who is strong.

Lost And Found...

first, i got lost
in his eyes, and in his words,
and in his arms holding me...
then i got lost in all the lies he told,
and i was just... *lost.*

but then i looked myself
in the eyes, and i started to find my voice,
and i learned to hold myself up,
and i began searching for my truth,
and now... i'm finding my way,
and i'm finding m*yself.*

she's learning to stop
bleeding herself out for others.

to *stop*. bleeding love. for those who
only drain her.

to let it all flow back to her...
to let all that love fill her own heart.

little by little
i'm learning to love myself.

and it might be *slow,*

but i'm certain in letting go of
all the things that tell me i shouldn't.

i've been letting go
of heavy things

sometimes the healing
isn't as complicated as it feels,
it just asks for space, and surrender, and release...

allowing time to turn the pages
and the memories to fade,
just letting all those messes untangle
and what's gone to fall away

grace...

learning to let things be
not meant for me

let yourself
find peace with the
apology that's never coming…
even if it came,
it wouldn't be enough,
and it doesn't hold your healing

i love like flowers and fire...
i don't know any other way.
soft and vulnerable,
and wild and burning...
with my heart broken. wide. open.
and even though he came in like wildfire,
he was just. broken.
and hardened. and filled with an
ugliness raging inside of him
and he thought that if he raged
hard enough against me
that he could rage an ugliness out
from inside of me too.
then he could say, "see, it's you."
that he could be so hard to love that
he could make me feel hard to love too.
but i just softly left the room.
a graceful exit.
and i wrote all my feelings down to shed
his hardened residue.
and to remind myself of all the ways
that there are such beautiful and tender
things in me... always.

exit gracefully.
heal and grow.
don't look back.

don't look for your
peace in getting back at them,
or trying to make them see your worth
and what they lost in you...

go more into yourself.
become a more beautiful, whole,
confident version of you...
one that doesn't need anything
from them to feel free.

- self-sovereignty

i promise,
once you learn to love
who you are,
it won't hurt anymore...
all of this pain from the one
who didn't love you.

you will love you, so it just
won't matter anymore.

....

Even if I'm slow to get there, the healing process *always* takes me back to myself. It guides me to give myself what others withhold from me, to heal myself where they have caused pain, to build myself up where they've tried to break me down, and once I start to give myself the things I need, what anyone else does or doesn't do for me or to me, no longer has power over me.

A Good Thing...

i think it's a good thing,
how we can struggle in such desperation
for clarity and still never find a way to make
any sense of how they treated us...

i think it means we're just not capable of
that same cruelty within ourselves.

and i think that's a really good thing.

on forced forgiveness...

not everything finds peace through
forgiveness. it just doesn't. and trying to force
something you don't authentically feel can
not only keep you from healing, but it can also
be a reinjury to your spirit.

sometimes you just feel it in you,
how forgiveness is asking too much of you,
and it's not because you're holding on, it's because
sometimes the burden of that shift,
that closure, that resolution, it isn't your work.
it's the other person's energy to move, and you cannot
move energy for others.

with those things, let it be ok that all they ask of you
is to breathe through and release.

breathe easy now...
you don't have to carry other
people's heavy anymore

i forgive you...
for treating me the way you
felt about yourself

he wanted me to feel
jealousy towards her, but i didn't,
i just felt compassion for her...

i too had once known the devastating
lack of self-love required to be with him

it was just
this quiet moment of
indifference to your existence...

and that's when i knew
that i had healed.

and when
i write this out,
this isn't to remember you...
it's to take it away
from you,
i'll take all these feelings i felt
and i'll make art,
i'll make something beautiful,
i'll make something new

- the alchemy in poetry

write it out
until what hurt you heals

therapy

this is heart work,
and you can't think your way
around this...

you've gotta feel your
way through it

just breathe,
and stay here in your peace

take time

to cleanse,

to heal,

to renew,

to grow,

to become.

keep letting go
of all of these things that
hurt to hold on to...

let it all fall through your fingers
until you feel free

...to just let it all be unheavy

i stood there
in front of you
and i thought of everything
that had ever broken me,
i thought of everything
that had ever shattered my heart,
and in that moment when i looked at you
i thought of how maybe
i'll tell you someday.
but for now, i just exhaled.
and i spoke nothing of any of it…

because all
of it made sense now,
and none of it
mattered anymore.

i hope that one day
the person who hurt you sees you from afar
dancing in the radiance of
your unburdened spirit and standing
strong in your fully mended bones...

and that for just a moment you feel their gaze,
so you can forever know, *without question,*
the powerlessness of their
perception over you

never be ashamed
of how deeply and passionately
you loved someone who destroyed you,
because destroying things is just who they are...

but loving things deeply and passionately
is *who you are*

the way you are...
how much you feel,
how you move, how you love...
you are such light. such *brilliant light.*
you are meant to be with someone
who is shifted by you,
whose soul is here to be shaken by you,
don't waste one more tender breath
that you have in your chest on
someone who was only ever there
to break your heart.

we may have

these fragile hearts,

and when we crumble,

ever do we crumble,

but unlike those who break us...

we heal

we grow

we become full

we rise

we thrive

and we fly

and
what if
you just hold on,
and what if life
holds so much more
than you can see
right now

i can feel it...
how i'm on my way,
to somewhere different,
something better than this

and i'll let it be light,
and new, and undiscovered

love

why else love
if not to feel stars
exploding in our veins

let yourself
fall into this wild love

you are everything
i could ever dream of...

come here knowing that nothing here
will ever tell you different

this love
like summer...
this light, this warmth,
how with you
it all feels so free

you feel like home,
and everywhere i've never been,
all at once

i don't know why it is, but...
you feel like home,
and everywhere i've never been,
all at once.
it doesn't make sense...
or maybe it does?
maybe love is the safest place you could ever be,
and every new and undiscovered place
you have yet to go,
all at the same time.
yeah...
i think that's perfectly how it's
supposed to feel.

there's this
beating in my heart,
and it sounds like you.
and this ache. in. my. chest...
it feels like *you.*

and in
every life
we fall like stars
into each other's skies
and we dream
our way
into each other's
destinies

when i look at you,
the way all my senses shift,
the way my soul sways...
it's how i know.

i just know...
it's soft next to you.
it's safe if i come close.
and there's destiny here,
there's meant-to-be
in your hands.
and you don't have
to say a thing,
it's in the way i'm shifted...
you just walk in,
and my heart beats different.

where there are walls,
you soften me.

i love in that
whole heart kind of way...
and you've got me
in that whole heart kind of way

you are
the sweetest
feeling i know

may my heart
be the softest place you fall,
may this love
be the wildest place you run

where
my heart is,
is where my mind
wanders,
and where my
body goes

everything,
all of me, always,
and only, and again...
it all finds its way
to you

you're an instinct.

- *loveflow*

i want to
tangle with you,
and fall into you,
and feel all of you,
your breath, your skin,
your hands, your heart,
your everything...

all of it, all of you,
all around me

i want to know
where that wild in your heart
wants to take me

show me your innerverse

i love
this feeling
with you...
how you ask me
to go higher

my soul just wants to be
closer to yours

he is
so beautiful,
but i love in energy,
so let me tell you of
just how
beautiful *he feels*

you are like golden hour,
it all glows different when
you're here

but *this*... this is something more,
it's some sort of holy thing, a sacred thing
...this love.

how you look at
me makes me wonder…
where do i belong *if not right here.*
right next to you.
breathing in all the life
under these stars until this
world ends

burn out the stars with me

i can't say them.
~~i can't say those three words.~~

i can't say it *in* three words…
i can't speak these things small.
i don't feel these things ordinary.
and i can't look at you and feel. these. things.
and fit them into predetermined patterns and
pre-ordered packages,
or practice how to speak them
in a rented ballroom,
or repeat them as a morning habit…
these are star things, and soul things,
and *all of my everything*, things…
so when you say…
do you, *will* you?
i *do*, and i *will*…
but out here where it's wild,
and up here where it's infinite,
and in me where i feel you,
where i've *always.* felt. you…
even before this. and where i'll feel you
after this, and beyond this…

so what i can't say means nothing.
and it means *everything.*

and what i mean when i say to you…
burn out the stars with me

…that's my way of asking for your forevers.

love me in a wild open
with a gentle hold

A Wild Open...

love me in a wild open
with a gentle hold
where i find myself, in myself
but let me feel
your racing heart
and your burning blood
through your steady hands
and let this be how we love
so we can love in a way that the stars we
come from want for us to know

let us burn and breathe all at once

inhale love fully, and let it breathe

he started to come closer,
and i said... *don't.* just stay. me here. you there.

he said... *so you don't want to know me.*

i said...
no, i do. let me know you. me here. you there.
not because i don't want to know you,
but, so i can know you as you are.
so beautifully untouched by anything you think
you need to make yourself to be for me.

please. *just be.*
let me love you as you are.

let me see
your chest bleed
and your heart ache
with all that you are
and for everything you love...

show me all your wildfires,
i want to know your wildfires

tell me how
the mountains give you peace
and the ocean makes you restless,
of the poetry you read
and the song you fall asleep with,
any fear that makes you bleed
and every dream that breaks you open,
this is what i want to know,
this is how my heart falls

what's in your head,
what's in your heart

i've never needed
for a dress or a ring,
but a hand held,
a promise kept,
a heartbeat felt,
a soul seen...
those are the things of
my everything

...the kind of boy who would
never break a pinky swear

his hands,
how they hold such
strong character...
it's why i fall into them
so softly

i knew it was him
by the way he walked in
wearing respect like a nice suit
and holding that
take
it
slow
magic,
with his self-love, self-required,
just radiating liberation from old men's tales,
and because...
before he'd let me love him,
it mattered
that i love myself

when my fears
ask why they should speak
softly around you,
i tell them...
your integrity tastes like sugar,
and that you carry goodness in
your hands like it
belongs

integrity is
the sweetest sugar

you are
so wildly beautiful
in all of the ways i could ever
imagine for someone
to be beautiful

how you weaken all of my defenses...
you're like a sweet kryptonite

the way you say
things to me, it makes me
want to know anything you have to
say about everything, really

...the way you speak, the things you know

i just get
captured by his vocabulary...

and it isn't in perfect grammar
or in fancy words,
but in *how*, and *why*, and *when*
he chooses words

there's just something
in the moments, and in the places,
and in the *because...*
and it's in this way that only he
does

it feels like... fingerprints,
or just this little glimpse into how,
and why, and *who he is.*

the way he looks at her...

as if her smile is the only thing
that could possibly matter

the way the
sunlight danced on her skin
and stardust lived in her eyes...
he knew he'd never want
to look away

love like flowers and fire

you are
a peace and a flame,
you steady me and stir me
all at once

every
little thing
feels so much softer,
so much sweeter,
with you.

the way
his voice sounds,
or the words he speaks...
i can just never decide what
pulls me in more

details,
i love madly in
details

that place
on the back of his neck
where my fingers fall
when my arms are wrapped around him
...that place.

details,
i love madly in
details

you are
this wilder way,
such a
sweeter touch...
some deeper place than
i've ever known

you give me fireflies

you smile like sunset,
one look at you and my
walls go down

as the summer sets in
and as this moment softens all
the fear between us,
there are only two things i need
to feel in this skin...

to be free, and to be
against yours

love me like wildfire

i just wanna
spend forever getting high off
what it feels like to be
around you

contact high

maybe we
could just kiss,
for hours,
like it's everything,
like it's art,
with no other
intention
but this

lay here
and lose time
with me,
let me tell you
of all the
things i adore
about you

there's that
corner of your smile,
the one towards me when you're
in the driver's seat...
how it lifts just a little when i say
something sweet

...add that to my favorite things.

how

your eyes

fall on me

so undistracted

undistracted

the way your
fingers fall in mine,
and how your heart is
racing wild,
and how my heart is
racing wild...
i just feel *so alive*

just let go of your head,
show me your heart
and run wild with me

go with me
everywhere in the world,
bare skin in sunshine,
lost under moonshine,
let's go

let's run free under
starlight

Road Trip...

just give me
your young, wild heart,
and i'll give you
my young, wild heart,
and we'll light up every city and
burn through every town
with how it feels

you and i...
we're meant to live in wild opens

summer air, freedom,
and *you*

like water,
and warmth,
this love
will hold you,
but it won't
hold you in place

love like breathing...

i think love is breath...
you breathe in, and come close,
and feel this, and feel me,
and feel it all,
and it takes you all in...
so you breathe out, and step back,
and feel you, and feel it all,
and take yourself in...
until you breathe in again

i think there has to be that breathing,
there have to be those exhales...
that space to take in new air and to
breathe back into yourself

i just think there's breathing,
i think love should feel like *breathing*

forever trying
to reconcile this hopelessly
romantic heart and this fiercely
independent soul

i'm such a soft lover...
and a wild wanderer

but i think you're where
all of me finds home

how you steady
this madness in my soul

the way he is
so sure within himself,
he never needs to make
me feel unsure...

it's beautiful the way a man's foundation
can let your heart call him home

nothing softens me
towards someone like the way
strength of character does

maybe there are
a few hard edges in you
and they just need a little soft touch,
and there are these tender places
in me that just need to know
this is a good love,
and maybe that thing i feel in the
way you take my hand...
how it's slow, but certain,
i think it's how we feel the light come in,
and maybe for just this moment
a little softness, and a little good love...
that's all we have to be.

- *trust fall*

close...

it holds
all these fears,
but all this softness,
in the most
vulnerable place
we ever know

there are
things he holds
close, in the awake,
in the lucid,
things he feels, but he fears
how they might fall out so helpless,
so unarmed, so defenseless...
and *god*, how those walls
can make me question.

but then he dreams with an open chest,
and he tells me of what he's sure of,
and that i can let my head rest,
'cause this isn't a small love,
and that most times it feels like too much love,
and so sometimes... he's just *afraid*.

and so my fears... they just fall quiet
with the way he speaks to me
in his sleep.

he may have a
hardened chest in the wake light,
but there are flowers in the moonlight,
and when his fears fall quiet...
there are all these things he feels
when his defenses are down.

in his sleep

pause

breathe

be here with me,

it's all i want,

it's all i need,

just this.

i don't need
fancy ways
and shiny things,
give me
slow hands,
honest eyes,
and full attention
with ease

...give me priceless things.

you have
such strong hands,
but my heart is such a soft thing,
so this could go one of two ways...

you could crush it
with the weight of all you are,
or maybe those strong hands could take
such a fragile thing
and hold it safe with the weight
of all you are

that *sure* kind of love...
where jealousy has no resting place,
and doubt has no home

it was the way
you just let me breathe here.
and just *be* here.
you didn't ask
anything else of me.
not to tangle in your weaknesses
or to heal your wounds.
you just asked me to know you...
to just *know you.*
to let it all be unheavy,
here next to you...
and just wonder of our dreams in
the glow of the moon.

in this moment
he just wanted to be in
this soft, sweet, wild, burning
existence of her

Moonglow...

where the light falls,
and the beautiful stays,
when the stars settle in...
come with me.

let's lose time

i want to melt
into you like wild honey,
you feel like summer sun

just to watch you
wear light on your skin
and trace peace in your fingertips...

how you smile at me
so easy.

- *summertime*

all
of these
beautiful
things

sunlight,
goodness,
stars,
you

give me love
that takes me wayward,
off beaten paths
and down country roads,
let's stargaze,
we're made for
so much more than plans
and picket fences

that late night drive,
make me a mixtape,
talk till 3am, stay up too late,
lay at the foot of your bed,
tell me what's inside your head,
wander my way through all the wonderful
ways of who you are,
kind of love

your beating heart, wild air,
and all the other things that make
me want to run free

meet me in that place
where our souls ache to wander
and a million stars will unfold around us
and i'll look at you and wonder
how we ever lived in anything
less breathtaking
than this

the way we
live forever young,
and the way we love...
how it feels like a forever love

we feel infinite

love like a timelapse of stars

through lifetimes...

until i die...
i will look at you and i
will feel this way until i die.
and then when i live again
i will feel this way, *still.*

may what you offer my heart
when we start
this dream
be evergreen
and expand
may no promise
rescind
with the wind
or time
may all you say is mine
be mine
...forever

now that i know you exist,
how do i not love you

you have
imprinted on me,
leaving traces of you here,
leaving light in my pathways,
it has shifted my soul,
and this life won't be the same...

i will not be the same

i feel you
like a breath on the air,
and in the light,
like a memory, or a dream,
or a sign of something,
in a hope for somewhere,
with a hold on anything...

i feel you everywhere,
i look for you in everything

if i don't
find you in this lifetime,
i will wait for you
until the next

i will wait for you until

it's always and ever
only *you.*

relationships & heartbreak

but if it's love...
when it asks you to come along,
it will not ask you to leave
yourself behind

people say they want love,
but they go into relationships asking...

what can you do for me?
what can i get out of you?
who can you be for me?

that's need. and i just think love is
something different. i think it asks different
questions. i think it looks for different things.
like...

what is this feeling with you?
what can unfold between us?
i want to know who you are.

a heavy relationship
isn't the same as a deep love...
a deep love won't weigh you down,
it will breathe into your soul and
allow you to be free

i want a love that as deep
as it feels it breathes
just as free

what if we don't ask this
to burden bear,
or heavy lift, and sift
through pain,
maybe we can do our own work,
so breath, and romance,
and what we taste like in every
color of love
can be what fills this space

- *intimacy*

....

One of my favorite things anyone has ever told me is that "*relationships are a reflection of the people in them.*" Meaning that whatever a relationship looks like, is just a combination of the energies of the people who are part of it. It felt so obvious when it was said to me, but I also feel like people rarely live as if that's so. We tend to not take responsibility for what our relationships look like. As if the relationship is something happening to us, rather than something we're co-creating. As if it's some separate entity that we have no say in or power to shape. But really, our relationships are pieces of who we are as individuals intertwining with each other.

It could feel confronting to see it that way, but I love to see it that way. For me, it means that my relationships don't have to be bound by patterns or limitations. They can be filled with as many beautiful ways as we are willing to be in them, and with as many beautiful things as we are willing to give to them.

When I wrote this poem, I was thinking of how often people say "relationships are hard," or "relationships are work," as if that's the default nature of our connections. But I'm passionate about a belief that it isn't. I think underneath it all, hard relationships are mostly a reflection of what the people in those relationships ask them to be. So, if we go into a relationship and we expect the other person to fix us, to fill us, to save us, to carry our weight, or to sort out our internal issues... then that relationship is going to *be work.* We are going into it making the choice of asking it to *do our work.*

I fully understand that many people feel that's what romantic relationships are for. And that's ok, too. I think we should be allowed to have different beliefs about what "relationship" means. But I also think that people who feel that way can often have a disconnect that their belief systems about romantic love are *why* their relationships are so much work. And they maybe don't allow for a different way to be possible.

I don't mean to say that relationships are perfect or without challenges. But instead of work, I guess I see a connection with someone else as being something that asks us for consciousness, and intention, and choice from within ourselves, and then the relationship flows from that. So, my "work" is in who *I* am and who *I* want to be... and then in *love,* to not ask the other person to be responsible for that.

I think that way of being can give us so much more freedom to experience beautiful things with someone. When we don't go to someone to *need* and *take,* we can *want* and *give,* and discover, and create... and just *love.*

i'm here... wanting
to know the shape of you,
without having to lose my own.
but just not yet knowing how...

how to take you in, *but keep me too.*

how to breathe love and wholeness
all at once.

to be
close to you...
the most
tender and
terrifying place
i know

stop listening
to the voice that tells you
that love is supposed to be hard,

it keeps leading you to places where
love ends up being hard.

codependency
doesn't keep you warm...
it keeps you from breathing
fresh air

it's just never been in me
to avoid loneliness with another
and try to call it love.

that person whose
broken pieces fit into
your broken pieces isn't the one

they may keep the bed warm,
but they're keeping you from whole...
just pretending that being broken
feels like home

and you can only romanticize
bad habits for so long,
before the ache to *yourself*
calls you home

one of the saddest connections is the
rebound relationship.
you're using one person to try to
unlove another.

there's nothing pure or honest
in what that relationship is,
or ever will be as you've carried into
it an unhealed bond to what was.

take time to cleanse,
to heal, to renew, to grow, to become.

what you go to just
because you're lonely isn't love,
what you're drawn to when you're
in your light...

that's where you'll find love

i watch everyone
move so fast
towards each other
and i think...
how beautiful it is
when it moves slow,
and takes time,
when it's curious,
how it lingers,
all those layers to uncover,
how it feels to explore

- *wanderlust*

i'm just
too in love with love
for anything less
than that heart racing,
soul craving,
lose my breath,
and feel my infinity
in the beating of your chest
kind of love

when you can feel
the remarkable, uncommon
texture of your soul,
you can't imagine letting anyone close
who isn't perfectly meant to
intertwine with it

i don't want to
search through all those other souls
trying to find some way to feel...

i just want to feel your soul.

i only know
how to crave
skin against skin
and my heart against
a chest
like a fingerprint

i need the grace of it,
this honesty within myself,
so it has to be a home...
even if you might not be careful here.

- *vulnerability*

i'm certain i love
with the entire force of the universe
and it feels too much to ask another
human to take that in

too much

how soft
my heart is...

it just isn't made for how
flawed humans love

it makes it harder to love people
when you won't let yourself
have faith in them

sometimes
we love
in fingertip touch...
and it's
just as close as
we can get

this is
aching... *and*
this is hope.
staring out at the
nashville skyline,
and wondering
where you are,
and if your skyline is just
as beautiful,
and does it hold all these
promises of us too

i will
look for you
in every lifetime,
until we finally stay

and when it ends...
i don't know if there's anything
harder to let go of than the way a song
makes you feel about them

- *when a music lover loves*

when you love,
the music around you becomes
the soundtrack to the stories you are living
with that person in them

that time, *those* places, *those* moments,
it intertwines with all of it.
it becomes the energy that captures what you
feel with them, what you feel *for* them.
it becomes this visceral, *engraved* part of the life you live,
the life you *know*... a life that has them in it.

so, when it ends...
when you have to start unweaving
them from your stories, and untangling them
from your energy, and unraveling. them. from. your. life.

out of everything you have to let go of...

i don't know if there's
anything harder to let go of
than the way a song makes you
feel about them.

- when a music lover loves

....

I've been in two relationships, and music was so incredibly intertwined in both of them.

My first boyfriend was a DJ. We met when I was still a senior in high school, and he was two years older than me, so for the first year, we were just friends... or something like it. I had a really toxic family life growing up, and that year it all kind of came to an explosive breaking point. During the fallout, he ended up becoming like a big brother to me, like family. But more than family, like *soul* family. And after I turned 18, he became even more to me. He was my first kiss, my first love, my first everything. He had grown up far more unsheltered than I had. I was this Southern girl whose life at that time was mostly cheerleading, and church, and Friday Night Football. He was this kid from the West Coast who was raised by a free-spirited hippie mama, and they had traveled and explored his whole life. So, he was like an awakening for me. And because he was a DJ, he *filled* my world with music.

When he wasn't making me playlists, he was always taking me to festivals and parties where he was working. Music connected us and surrounded us. It was the heartbeat of who and what we were together. That time with him was a really magical time of self-discovery for me. We were so wild and curious and free... and for a while, we were really, really beautiful to each other.

But I was still so young and so lost. I just didn't have any idea of who I was at all. I was running away from a lot of things that were going on inside of me, and so I did a lot of running away from how I felt about him, and from how he felt about me. He was still young and unsure of who he was, too, so he had his own ways of destroying things. And we both broke each other's hearts. And when it ended, I had an entire music library I couldn't touch for a while. I just couldn't listen to much of anything and not think of him. Not only had he introduced me to so much music, but those songs had also been so intertwined with the moments that we had intertwined with each other.

And as I healed from that heartbreak, I remember the music feeling like some sort of progress marker of my healing. As I could take songs in again and not feel the same, it felt like it was because I was growing and changing. I was just no longer the same person who had felt all those things from before. The music felt different, and so did I.

And the second relationship, he was a singer in a band. Music was *everything* in his world. I was still really unsure of who I was, and didn't have a hold on my own world. As with the first relationship, there was music everywhere around us, too. I would go to his shows, or we would spend time up at a cabin where his band was recording, or we would go on these long drives where we would listen to each other's playlists for hours. And while there were a lot of things that felt really beautiful with him too, there was a lot of destruction and heartache with him more than anything. And when it ended, it was chaotic and painful, and I was left with so much confusion and no sense of closure whatsoever. But this time I didn't run from the music, I drowned in it. Some of it was his music, so it was more than just music... it was pieces of him. And I think I did this thing where I let the music completely romanticize that relationship into something it never really was. And I think healing from him was a lot slower because of it. Some songs are just barely becoming safe again, and some songs maybe never will be.

And I think that's just how powerful music can be. It's such an aesthetic in our existence. We *feel so much* from it, and because of it, and through it... and so it can break us completely open in heartbreak, but I wouldn't trade that for how much it makes us feel alive and free and infinite, and *in love*, in all of the beautiful moments.

the spaces we've called love...

it's heartbreaking
how many of us have felt *in love*
with people who were not even kind
to us...

how many of us weren't taught that
love can't exist in a space without kindness.
or without respect. or in a space that
doesn't honor us and cherish us.

so many of us are learning that the spaces
we've called being *in love,* weren't
spaces of love at all

The Beautiful Things They Do...

if you keep trying to find love
with people who are broken inside
you will spend your energy and the moments
of your life, *so* lost, searching for understanding
of why they do all of the harmful, destructive
things they do...

but if you can be patient with love,
and save yourself for a love
with someone who is whole within,
then you will get to live your moments
and spend this journey endlessly in awe of the
way they do all of the stunningly
beautiful things they do.

the in-between...

sometimes a soul
needs a growing space,
a before space or an in-between
to go within...
but you can't ask someone
to be a forever waiting for you
if you're trying to fill
that in-between space with
other temporary faces

patience with a soul searching and pain from
an ego seeking... it's not the same thing.

but if he
was right for you...
it would break his heart open
to see you hurt in the very
way he hurts you

....

This is so unquestionably one of the biggest lessons in my own growth... that if you have to reconfigure or recolor who someone is to you or how they treat you to try to make it look like love, then *it isn't love.* It's taken me a lot of unlearning to *truly* understand this... to understand that trauma bonds are not destinies, that people who are meant for me will be good for me and good to me, and that the kind of pain that others have caused me is the very kind of pain that someone who is meant for me would never want me to know.

sometimes what you feel
about someone just isn't enough.

it just isn't.

because what they feel about themselves
will try to destroy what you feel about yourself
if you get close to them.

some people are
convinced they've been
hurt by you simply because you've
stopped letting them hurt you

you will
hurt her, and rage
against her, and completely push
her away, and once she's gone...

you're going to find that this war was
inside of you all along

- the mirror

you say it aches,
how much you miss her...
but did you love her with an ache when you had her?

you had every bit of her full attention,
but where was yours?
she broke her heart open for you
again and again... and you *just. kept. closing yours.*

and so you lost her. and now you learn...
you learn that holding has to have wanting,
and appreciating, and valuing. you learn that love
isn't static. it's kinetic, it's movement,
it's growth and curiosity. you learn that ~~there has~~
~~to be just as much~~ *there has to be more* wanting in the holding
than there is in missing, or in reaching for.

you learn that you have to ache for people when it matters...
you have to love someone when you have them.

there is a man
who will give her all the
love you withheld from her...
and she *will* find him

she's not coming back.

a 4-word story for the boy
who mistakenly thought she'd never
realize her worth and walk away

and if you
took me for granted...
you must know that *that*
was another life.
and i have found my way
to a new life.
and you are just not welcome here.

because i can no longer
wear that shade of unworthiness,
or hold that self-unkindness,
that let me live a life
where the people i let close to me
ever treated me as anything less than
a blessing in theirs.

and if you wonder where i went...

i walked away
because i couldn't feel
all of the beauty and goodness
and wonder and light in me
if i stayed close to someone who
wouldn't let me feel it

for so long
i wanted you to hold me
until i realized how small you
needed me to be to fit within
your grasp

you don't *love,*
you just hold people close
to have someone to hurt,
or to hurt someone else with...

but none of it's love.

Drive...

you used to
drive me everywhere,
and nowhere, for hours,
just so we could talk
about everything, and nothing,
for what felt like forever...

but then you drove this nowhere,
and you left nothing

....

He would come pick me up and take me out somewhere, and then after we went wherever we went, he just wouldn't want to take me home. And I just wouldn't want to go home. So he would just *drive.* Sometimes around the edges of town, or out on some backroad, or up into the hills. He'd put a playlist on and he'd just *drive.* And we'd just talk, for hours, about nothing, and about everything, and about anything else in the universe that came up. Sometimes we'd end up pulling over for a sunset on a random interstate turnout, or we'd stop in some small town at some late night diner, or sometimes we'd even drive so far and for so long that we'd end up watching the sunrise in some new place we'd never been.

The playlist in the background, the stars outside the windows... we'd just *lose time.*

Everything about it was just *pure.* Neither of us needing or taking anything from each other, no human traumas, no acting out our wounds, no one hurting anyone... just two people completely lost in curiosity about each other's existence.

I will never know him again. Those drives we took were only part of our story, and he ended up being an unimaginable heartbreak in my life. But I still hold special the things I felt on those drives with him. And I don't mean what I felt *for him,* but what I felt with him. That feeling of wanting to just take in someone's soul energy and lose time with them, with no other agenda.

I think even when we leave someone behind, we can take some of the things we felt with them forward with us. Just as things that we feel are beautiful about love. And I think for me, out of all the things we feel from love, there's nothing more beautiful than wanting to just be in each other's existence.

all those pretty things...

the way you would say such
pretty things to me, i took it in like air,
but you were so careless with special things,
and it left me here...

so
unable
to breathe.

and after
everything,
you won't even
grant me
the smallest mercy
of your absence
from my memory

i spent all that time
haunted by the ghost of
someone you never really were

to be able to let go of you
it feels as if i'd also have to let go
of who *i've* been
...but i think that was your purpose.

- the catalyst

i finally stopped waiting...
waiting for him to feel sorry, to feel regret,
to feel guilty, to realize how much he had lost
in me and to feel some certain way for all
that he had done to me

i finally understood...
it really never had anything to do with me.
someone who is capable of all
that he had done was just never capable
of feeling anything at all.

....

Though I didn't know that's what he was at the time, I grew up the child of a narcissist. And so, it's no surprise that the kind of man that my daddy was is the kind of man I ended up in a relationship with. Because witnessing dysfunction your whole life doesn't necessarily make you able to recognize it. If anything, it makes you unable to see it because it's all been normalized in front of you for so long.

So, when I was recovering from that relationship, it was a shock to my system to realize that what I had always believed was "love," just wasn't love at all. And it wasn't until after I walked away from him that I even learned what a "narcissist" was. Once I did, everything about him, and my daddy, it all finally had a tangible description. And with me being someone who feels everything to *such depths*, it was a brutal lesson in life to realize that there are people who just don't feel any of it at all.

When you feel everything so deeply, it's just sort of unfathomable in your understanding that someone can be *so* different from that. That someone can be so unfeeling, and controlled, and compartmentalized... and so unapologetically unkind. And you can try desperately to look for some sort of spark of that same kind of piercing blood flow that you carry inside of you, but instead, you just find layers of cold ego. They only "feel" when they are either losing control of something or losing access to something they want to keep having access to. And so they only "feel" when their ego is losing the things that feed it.

It's just an incredibly heartbreaking understanding to grasp. The idea that they're just not even capable of the very things that drive your existence. But it's also the understanding that finally brings you peace. You stop looking for what you "did wrong" because you start to see that how they are just isn't about you. And you stop losing your mind chasing for answers and trying to make sense of it. You start to realize that it's not a way of being that is ever supposed to make sense to you.

And maybe underneath it all, somewhere on a soul level, hiding beneath their layers of human traumas and ego wounds, they are capable. But it's *their* journey to find it. And your journey isn't meant to be wasted on being destroyed by them in the meantime.

he gave me every
reason not to believe in love...
yet here i am after everything,
so *beautifully* certain it exists

someday i'm going
to love someone, and i'm going
to lay at their feet more love than they
could've ever imagined

...and you will never be anything
more to anyone than somebody that
someone, somewhere is
recovering from

we cannot curse the sky
if we stay and break bread
with boys
and their troubles
while men full of mountains and moons
are waiting with stories of
how far they've come

a wild heart burning...

you stay still
waiting for a cold heart to
warm towards you,
while somewhere else out there
is a wild heart burning,
so untamed, and so unafraid to light up
everything in you

when they
are meant to love you,
they would have to fight it to not feel it...
it will be in their stars

everything in you
is meant to be felt by someone
who loves as raw in their nerves
and as full in their blood,
and could never be unaffected by you

-*fire*

people who love
passionately are meant to
be loved passionately

there's this
way a woman can be
free to want you, to fall into you,
so intensely, so passionately,
when she can feel it from you...

how she's everything you want

the person you are meant
to be with will be fascinated by you...

completely and breathtakingly
fascinated by you.

truly faithful fades no
measure with company or
circumstance.

when someone
is meant for you
faithful will be effortless,
like a destiny,
like a way of being
that only you make sense in,
like a journey you hold endless
stories for

wait for this.

....

I feel like this poem has to be given a deeper explanation because I'm not sure that what I meant fully comes through, and so I think where this came from within me matters. One of the things I'm most incredibly passionate about in life is a fierce belief in the individual journey. A fierce belief that every soul is here to experience something unique to their soul's DNA. And that includes the way we each experience relationships. What our relationships look like, what makes us fulfilled or happy within them, and how we want to experience connection... I'm passionate about the idea that there is no one singular box or template that we're all supposed to fit into. And I think some of the most painful suffering we go through as humans can come from not listening to our soul within our relationships and connections, including not honoring what kind of connection feels right for us.

So, all of that being said, this poem wasn't meant to judge anyone.

I understand that not everyone is made for or even interested in monogamy. I also think there are many different versions of monogamy, and that what monogamy looks like for one person can be very different for the next. I think what matters is that each person within a connection is not only honest about what "connection" looks like for them but also that each person is experiencing and being given the kind of connection and commitment that is right for their soul... whatever that is.

For me, monogamy is the only thing that has ever felt right. I've just never had "casual" in me. But at the same time, the way many people experience monogamy has never captured what feels right for me either. Not because I'm *not* drawn to a faithful connection, but because *I am*. Intensely, passionately... the kind of thing that carries through lifetimes. But I've always been searching for something beyond the boxes and patterns that we're told we have to fit ourselves into. I've always been searching for something that doesn't have to restrict or struggle to hold its energy. The kind of connection where being faithful is effortless because it's something that's soul driven.

The idea that being faithful is *work*, or a duty, or something that we force upon ourselves just so we "don't hurt the other person," that has always felt awful to me. If it's something we have to force, then are we truly happy? Shouldn't love be a place where we are our most fulfilled, and our most *free*? I think many of us want that, a kind of fidelity that's magnetic and *unforced*. Something that comes from an organic place.

So, that's what I was trying to express when I wrote this, an idea of a "higher" version of monogamy. Something beautiful and expansive and free. And also something that you never feel like you have to fight for or beg for. And at the time that I wrote this, I was sort of coming into a powerful realization that I had been settling for less than this in my life. That I had let others make me feel as if what I wanted was too much, or not possible. And what I was beginning to understand within myself, is that there has never been anything wrong with the kind of connection and commitment that I crave. The only thing that was ever wrong was me letting other people put their own limitations or shortcomings onto me.

Also, when I wrote this, I think I hoped that these words would maybe be comfort and encouragement for anyone else who has been settling for less, or who has let their own ideas of love be discouraged by other people's limitations or treatment of them. I think whatever it looks like, the kind of love we believe in exists... and we know it does because it's within *us*. And since we suffer when we don't honor it, I think that makes it worth waiting for.

you'll know...

not just in the way they look at you,
but in how they're not looking
anywhere else

who you dream of being,
and who your soulmate dreams
of being with...
it will be the same thing.

....

I believe that true love doesn't just give us the space to be the best version of ourselves, but that it also could never be a space where we feel like we are not enough for the other person. I just don't see how it could ever feel like *love* to live your life in a space where you feel *not enough.* I think that when it's the *highest* kind of love, there's divine alignment between your self-love journey and your soulmate connection. And that if you genuinely go towards your best version, and the other person still wants someone else or something different than who you are, then they're just not your person. And when someone is meant for you, the *"you"* you dream of being, and the *someone* that they dream of being with... it will all be the same thing.

your heart
is being prepared
for the heart
that is being prepared
for your heart

patience.

he said...
"it's a long walk home",
but i never could've known just
how far we would roam...
how long i'd have to hold on.

i think
it's been his soul
passing through the others...
leaving traces of him,
of these memories we've yet to live,
leaving breadcrumbs to him
in the ones who were
just lessons,
it's been breadcrumbs to home...
all of it guiding me as i grow.

i know you...
you're in my stars

and you say we'll find a way...
promise me we'll find our way

connection

my soul
just thinks your soul
is pure magic

i could get lost
in all the little ways
you carry love, and carry light,
and hold so much
goodness in your being,
you are a golden thing
in this heavy, heavy world,
and everything feels new
when i look at you

i just like your way,
the way you feel, how you are,
who you are... i'm just drawn to you.

some people's
very existence inspires
you to dream

one of the
sweetest ways to love...
i'll let you grow

sometimes,
love people easy
like fine, light rain
be there
but with breathing room
and growing space
asking for nothing
but the glow in their skin

maybe sometimes
we're delicate, and unsure,
and we don't know what we're ready to want,
so all that we're really looking for
are people with good intentions towards us...

hoping for gentle in the unknown

when you can
trust that every word
a person says to you is true
you can *feel it in your bones,*
how it's safe to just believe in them.

and there's nothing in the world
like that feeling...

good intentions are like magic.

i think i melt from authenticity
more than anything

Journey Companions...

please let
everyone on my journey
be kind and good to my heart and soul,
and please let anyone who isn't
easily pass through.

we honor the
people around us by taking
responsibility for our own energy,

we honor ourselves
by choosing to have people around us
who are willing to do the same.

we cannot
carry another
on their own way...
in soul searching,
we must all find
our own legs beneath us,
our own voice inside of us,
and our own
light to guide us.

and if you are in darkness,
and if they come to you,
and if they reach a hand down
to pull you out,
be sure that if you take their hand
you do not drag them into the dark,
but go with them...

go with them into the light

you remind me
what heaven's air felt like...

i think you're here to
walk me home

my heart
is tethered
to a soul
i've always known,
in a person
i've yet to find

imprint.

we have the same kind of
stardust in our souls

we love like fireflies,
how we gravitate to each
other's glow

we're here
with all this chemistry
in our veins,
so let's stay up
and talk
about heaven, and earth,
and of your dreams,
and my dreams...

and maybe you could come closer and
show me love-colored things

- *late night conversations*

how beautiful it feels
when they want to know
all about the worlds you hold
inside of you

i just like your soul aesthetic

the way you carry that energy
when you come close...

it's my undoing, *every time.*

eye contact and a lip bite

maybe i like
that you came here
to do more
than pass time, or hold your space
over there,
and i could trade my foothold
for my senses shaken,
and forgo my ability
to stay in my body,
if you want to show me
how abandon
can feel like magic

let go,
run wild with me

you feel like...
a *terrifyingly*
effortless fall

and i think
if i come closer
i would not recover
from you

and would i want to

...your beautiful gravity.

you walk in,
and my heart beats different

i am intensely
drawn to sincerity

it feels like
coming home after
being gone for too long
the way i gravitate to
the good in you...

how i just crave
that *goodness* in you.

you steady me and stir me
all at once

this way you
so gently, yet confidently
ask me to grow,
you are flowers and fire
so softly, yet knowingly
awakening me
to all of these things
i want to become

- *spring*

we are
not halves of
each other,
we come here to
love the whole of
one another

you turn these still
places into breathing,
this. warm sun... how it wakes
a motion

you take this feeling in me
and turn it into a high road,
and an open life

you can't come here and ask me
to feel all this love, and not turn it
into the shape of you...
you make everything beautiful,
everything about you is
made of soul

and you say we'll find a way...
promise me we'll find our way

i just like how it
feels when you're here,
and maybe that's all i know

you soften me.

he said,
close your eyes for just one moment
and imagine...
what if everything you fear is an illusion,
and all these things you dream
are what is real

he wanted me to believe in the universe

....

I was raised in a home with an enormous amount of fear energy. Fear was a constant in the environment, in the way we were treated, and also in the beliefs we were taught. And I absorbed all of it. So, not long after I left home, I started having panic attacks because I had buried so much of that energy inside of me. And I didn't know what the attacks were at first. My heart would just start racing out of nowhere, and then the entire world would spin out of control.

This poem was about a night when I was with my first boyfriend, and one of those panic attacks started to overtake me. He was incredibly energetically intuitive so, even though I'd never talked to him about the panic attacks before, when one began happening that night, he just instinctively knew how to help me. He took my hands and told me to close my eyes. Then he told me to take deep breaths and to let myself imagine that what was happening to me was just fear. And as I calmed down a little, he told me to start telling him about all of the things I was afraid of. At first, I couldn't say anything, but eventually, the fears started spilling out of me. And he held my hands as I breathed through all of it.

He told me that it was ok to put those fears down. And then he told me that it was ok to let myself imagine something different. And he said that if I could imagine something different, then my world could be different. I had grown up believing in a universe that wanted me to be afraid, and he wanted me to believe in a universe that loved me. And that kindness from him completely settled the madness in my soul that night.

We are no longer in each other's lives, but I'll carry that night, and other things from him with me forever. That night alone was a big step in my journey of learning to go inward for answers and a sense of peace. Because of him, my life won't be the same... *I won't be the same.*

maybe we
could just lay here
and i could just
kiss your skin,
until you feel this light,
until beautiful settles
easy on you,
until all that love in you
feels like home

reach into
my heart through
the bones of my chest
and uncover it all...
feel anything that's there
and *breathe easy.*

- *the way honesty feels*

show me
all your wildfires...
i want to know your wildfires

what makes you feel…
what makes *you. feel. alive.*
how is your breath stolen.
how. and when.
does this life give you arrhythmia.
what pulls at you so much that it hurts
not to chase it.
the dreams out there, the hopes in here.
the art, the words, the songs…
what *shifts* you.
that somewhere beautiful in this world
that calls to you in the early light…
those aching things that keep you up
so restless after midnight.
what takes you higher than this world,
what takes you deeper into your soul light…
all of those things…
i want to *know. those. things…*
show me all of your soul things

i think maybe
i've already loved you
in a million different ways,
through different timelines,
and there's this way
we always, yet never align,
like we test this parallel, and run
before we collide

- the way souls dance

i feel you everywhere,
i look for you in everything

you're somewhere
in this world,
and i'm somewhere
else in this world,
and there's this
feeling in my soul,
and i hope it gets to you

just to know you're
somewhere in this universe

may we hold on to
the promises our souls make

humanity & society

how we treat people...
it matters.

i hope i make it a
little softer here for someone.

if i do but one thing today
may i be human sunshine
for someone

may my heart be broken
wide open with compassion

poetry is my scripture,
music is my gospel,
empathy and kindness are my witness,
creativity and love are my worship

hatred feels thick,
and noisy,
as if it imposes and takes up space.
but i have to believe it's just the absence of things...
like an emptiness raging against itself.
that it's no substance of power.
that it doesn't get to make a permanent home here.
and that those who harbor it are surely not powerful,
and that they don't control this space.
that love can always fill the air.
and if those who are hellbent on hate
won't grow, or change,
that awakened voices will bring revival
to this place.

no matter how loud or heavy that
hatred can rage, i have to believe it hasn't won...
and that love will always
outnumber, overshadow, and overcome.

....

In memory of Heather Heyer

we're not
meant to be
color blind...
we're meant to see
all this beauty,
all this texture,
all this life,
in every color,
and every kind

i just like good souls,
knowing them, being one,
it's kind of all that really matters

be a love firefly

if i could help
every woman feel beautiful,
and teach every little girl how to love herself,
that would be my superpower.

my superpower

woman to woman,
may we allow each other
the freedom to explore
all of the depths and variations
of our own femininity
and not judge or condemn each other
for the layers and directions
of womanhood
we each choose to pass by or take on.
we will not all find and define ourselves
in the same way,
but as we find and define ourselves,
let us not stand in each other's way.

young boy
you will grow
they will tell you to be strong
they will teach you to be tough
i hope someone tells you to feel
i hope they teach you to be love
young man
grown man
let yourself be love

....

This may seem as if it was written about a specific someone in my life because it feels intimate and personal, but this poem actually came to me in the middle of a college football game, lol. I was watching my Tennessee Volunteers play South Carolina a few years ago, and there was this moment where one of the QBs got sacked like a freight train. And after the sack, the camera panned into the QB's face as he got back up. He had this sweet, innocent face, and yet he was dusting himself right off like nothin' after just getting sacked like a freight train.

At that moment, I was *really* taken aback by the contrast of his sweet face with the brutality that had just been inflicted upon his body. It was a moment where it would've been entirely valid for any human being to break down and cry and want their mama, but he just stood right up, dusted himself off, and pressed on.

I just became overwhelmed with this thought process of how we ask so much of men in our society when it comes to "masculinity." We ask for so much "toughness" in moments where men should just be allowed to be human, and it broke my heart open. How with all of the things that we put into little boys' heads that are supposed to be "the measure of a man," we so often don't include their right to be vulnerable, and to *feel*, and to just *be human.* And we surely don't tell them enough that it's their right to *be love.*

So, this poem spilled out of me. And truthfully, I've struggled with a lot of pain from men in my life, and many of the things I've written have been about processing that pain. I've also written a lot in the other direction, about romantic love. With men, my writing has mostly come from pain or passion, but not very often from neutral places between those extremes. So when this poem came out of me, it felt like a healing moment. It felt so pure, and so filled with compassion, and without any agenda other than to just be kind. This poem will always hold a soft place within me because of that feeling.

misogyny is a weak man's crutch.

she's not here just to be
a supporting character in your story...

she has her own entire story
to live too.

i hope you know
you matter now
chosen by no one
belonging to yourself

i hope you go on
living in skin untouched by anything that your
sovereignty did not bless into your existence
and breathing air that holds no can'ts
and carries no words
of how a woman
should or should not be

- choices

let a woman
have her own worth.
let her value be found in *who she is.*
not in who she is to a man.
not in who she is to whom she supports,
or serves, or takes care of, or carries weight for.
not who she is in the context of anyone else's story.
just who she is. *as she is.*

bare,
alone,
unburdened,
beautiful,
and worthy.

soul

earth, fire, water, sky…
wild, soft, free… and full of flowers.
she makes everything beautiful,
everything about her is made of soul.

her wings unfolded

you hold entire
universes inside of you

Wildfire Heart...

it's breathtaking,
how your heart spills out of you
so achingly soft, and so chaotically unsure,
but as if the entire world catches fire
and you're wanting to just be
so in love with it all

her,
because she
makes life poetry,
she turns every bit
of it into art

you *are* beauty...
it radiates from the depths of your soul
to the tips of your toes

you are a golden thing
in this heavy, heavy world

you've got
this big heart
and it's full of all
these big dreams
and maybe sometimes
they feel too big
and maybe sometimes
it feels too hard
but the heavens want to have
favor on you
and it may take a long time
but it will happen in its right time
so take a deep breath
and just hold on

just hoping for gentle
in the unknown

...my heart is such a soft thing

some of us just aren't made
for how hard the edges are here,
for how slow pain moves,
or how lost light can get,
and how heavy it all can weigh...

we're surely not made for how flawed humans love.

but while we're here...
we can try to love a little deeper, and burn
a little brighter, and maybe, just maybe,
we make it a little softer
here for someone.

- *angels and earth*

Soft Soul...

you are so
sensitive, and you think
that's what's
wrong with you...
but it's something beautiful
about you,
it's what makes you
so good.

unfolding into yourself...
what a tender, delicate thing

patience with how your heart wanders,
you will find your way

your heart
tells you big things
in little ways...
listen.

are you fear
or are you love,
ask this of everything that wants
to be here with you

- thoughts, energy, and companions

clarity...

may this stillness stay
and quiet the noise in my head
so i can hear the voice in my heart

give it to the universe.

if it keeps you
up at 3am,
i hope you're
cultivating worth,
and nurturing patience,
and building pathways
that you find your way to
in the sunlight

- *purpose*

what you have...
it isn't here yet.
what you hold, what you are,
it's why you're here.

maybe you create, or shift and change,
or just love in a way this world doesn't know yet.
whatever that light is... it's your work here.

those things you feel in you
but don't yet see,
you're meant to breathe them
into being.

- lightwork

if this life doesn't
look like your soul feels,
keep going.

this world is
too wide
and this universe
is too big
and you are just
too beautiful
and there is just
way too much inside of you
for you to let this
be the end

The Turning Point...

let go your fear
as it falls
beautiful, be still
this untangling of it all
let your bones fill with might
let your lungs fill with free

don't look back.

i hope
you never
let the ones
who are
sleepwalking
hold you back
in your
own awakening

....

This is something that I have had to learn to be strong about in every area of my life. With the paths I've been taking on my spiritual journey, with the steps I've been taking in learning to love myself, in my relationships and energetic connections... in everything, really. You just can't let other people's unconsciousness hold you back in this life. Where they have limitations that are too small for you or beliefs that don't feel right for you, or where their vibration lowers your vibration... you just can't stay in places that you're growing out of. There's nothing wrong with where they are, for them, but we have to honor ourselves, and we ache inside on a soul level if we hold ourselves back in the places that we are awakening.

your heart
isn't made to settle...
you must choose the greatest love,
and you have to chase the
greatest life

why else
are we here if not
to live with unreasonable
passion for things

anyone who tells
you the fairytale isn't real
just hasn't found it yet,
or they settled for less, but that's
their story, not yours.

let yourself believe in your fairytale.

....

A lot of us grow up with other people's stories being forced onto us. What we're allowed to think, to feel, to want, to believe... it's decided for us and dictated to us. And it doesn't really matter if it feels right or wrong for us, we're not supposed to question it. If we have peace, or wellbeing, or a sense of self, *none of that matters.* We're just supposed to accept that life and love and reality are all limited to what other people tell us they are, and then live accordingly.

I grew up in that kind of world, and I was lost my whole life because of it. I wanted something different, I believed in something more, and it killed my spirit to push it down. So, a big part of my journey has been learning to be unapologetically defiant in giving myself permission to think, and feel, and want for, and believe in what feels right *for me.* Whether it's what I believe about love, or spirituality, or just life in general, to be relentlessly protective about what I hold and nurture in my inner world. Whenever someone tells me that something isn't possible, or realistic, or right, or says that it's just "not the way things are," I don't give it any more weight than it being their personal beliefs for themselves.

I'm learning more and more to value my internal compass over anything outside of myself. So, if some sort of hope, or dream, or life vision, or *love* vision exists inside of me, I feel like it's been put there on purpose. And it just doesn't matter what anyone else believes, I honor it, and I let myself believe in it.

let yourself

have faith in things

when we let go of
the need to control it all
think the universe listens...
instead of our old patterns we'll
get spark-starters and soul awakeners,
and instead of the hard lessons we'll be given
inspirers and spirit challengers

...and maybe it's as simple as to just *be curiosity.*

....

This is maybe one of the most uncertain things I've ever written. By that, I mean, I don't know if I knew how to say what I was trying to say when I wrote this. I had a sense of what I was feeling and wanted to express, but I didn't totally know how to articulate it, so this will always feel a little awkward to me.

I think I was just thinking about how we can get so caught up in trying to control things in our lives - outcomes, relationships, experiences - all of it. We either want things to go a certain way, *or* we're scared that things will end up going a certain way. So, we put all this energy out into the universe that projects our worries, our past experiences, our fears, and even a desperation. And I guess I believe that it can affect who and what comes to us in our lives.

That the energy we're putting out can sort of pull us into repeating old patterns, or cause us to block new experiences. And I think when we let go of that need to control everything, and we just let ourselves be *curious* and have a willingness to allow things, we move into more open spaces with different possibilities. Instead of spaces where our fears unfold, we move into more spaces where our hopes can.

i haven't felt
what i'm meant to feel,
i have not loved
who i'm meant to love,
i haven't yet been
who i'm meant to be...

not yet.

there
are times
that my faith
gets weary
from the
aching in my back
where my wings have
yet to grow

- *the butterfly process*

a persistent yearning
to feel at home in this skin,
to feel my soul
grounded in these bones

someday
you will look
at yourself,
and you'll see in you
all these things
your soul is made of,
and you will
be home

who are you
when all of the things
that feed your ego
fall away

let things break you wide open,
that's where the golden light is

dear heart,
why do you run from the
things that give you a pulse

...don't fear what makes you feel

you close your heart
and you think it is a safety,
but it is a violence against yourself
in the quietest of ways,
yes, quiet, but still a violence,
a brutal, aching violence,
and to love, it is bravery,
and no small bravery,
but a fearless, grand reach into
an uncontrollable unknown,
yes, an uncertainty,
but maybe, what a beautiful unknown

forever trying
to reconcile a hopelessly
romantic heart and a fiercely
independent soul

a soft lover,

and a wild wanderer

wanting everything
and ready for nothing,
intense energy
and inconsistent energy
terrify me all the same

when both passion and fear
have you fully consumed...
this is what it is to have a heart born
in the soft light of the virgo sun
and a sagittarian spirit that dances
under a restless gemini moon

– the sun, the moon, and my heart

my heart,
oh how wild it loves

i love in heartbeats,
slow and sweet, *so* sweet,
and hard, and reckless,
and racing, and *so* close,
maybe too close...
so then running,
and reaching, and aching,
but in heartbeats, everything,
all of it, in heartbeats

the universe gave me
a relentlessly loyal heart,
i could love through lifetimes

she loves like an awakening

you make everything beautiful,
everything about you is
made of soul

the way your heart just
spills out of you

i keep
falling,
and feeling,
and loving too much,
but isn't feeling it all
existence

so achingly
desperate to believe
in myself, in life,
and in anything beautiful that can't
be crushed by something cruel

sometimes
it hurts in a way that
it feels like you hurt for everyone
who has ever hurt this way...
i think it's called *soul ache.*

a soft spirit
in a hard world.

dear soul,
if i had known it would be this hard,
i don't know if i would've come

- *human*

it's been really, really hard,
but you've been *so* brave.

hold on...
these things that tear
your soul apart will someday
be no more than a faded memory
with no hold on you

when you feel lost, look up...

just let all
the pretty lights in the sky
guide you home

....

Ever since I can remember, going outside and looking up at the stars has been one of the most powerful feelings in this world for me. Especially at times when this world doesn't feel like home, the stars have this way of reminding me of a home, *somewhere.* And I think a lot of people have that same feeling when they look up at the stars.

So, this is something my friends and I tell each other whenever we feel lost in life... if it feels like there are no answers, go outside, look up, and take in the stars. Let the pretty lights guide you home. There's just something in the night sky that helps us remember that we are more than our current human experiences. That we're on a soul journey. That no matter what we're going through in this human moment, it's a small, temporary moment. And no matter how big and overwhelming it all feels, someway, somehow, we're going to find our way home.

this world
will get heavy...

stay unshaken in pursuit
of the light

don't be afraid
to leave it all behind...
there is new light, and new life,
there are new worlds waiting

i want to fall
into that beautiful life
into the soft spaces
into the glow
where there's moonlight
where there's soul light
and where it means
something if you come close
and let your heart beat
against mine

you said,
tell me where you've been, love

and i thought of all the lost roads,
and dark corners,
and heavy work, and heartbreak,
and of all the healing

and i just said...
on my way here

spirit

there she was...
so beautiful and free

she has a wild spirit,
but a soft heart,
and such a sweet soul

lay here...
safe in the
morning light,
soft in the daylight,
until sunlight becomes
skin light,
breathe in and
let the flowers wrap
you up in sweet
until the air comes easy
from your chest,
until the sky becomes
something you can touch,
and the earth becomes
somewhere you can stay
and still have wings

i think you're made of flowers
how you bloom when there's light
on your skin

she's always preferred sunrises
over sunsets...
she likes beginnings

....

There's often a negative connotation around the idea of being in love with the beginning of things. An idea that the "honeymoon phases" of our experiences aren't as *real.*

But I love beginnings.

I love that feeling when something is new and undiscovered and full of so much possibility in front of you. It just makes me feel alive to be in those wide open spaces where things aren't yet planned out, those spaces meant for curiosity. I even appreciate the uncertainty in them.

I do also understand the value of endings. And I know that beginnings always shift into other phases, and *that's all ok.*

But I still passionately love the beginnings. And I think there can be just as much substance and value and beauty in an awakening of something as there is in a deepening. I don't think any of it is less real; I think it's all just different kinds of energy. In fact, I think too often people can miss the value in a beginning. They race towards the defined and the established, they push to the outcome, to the destination. They don't live in the little moments of the experience. They don't take in the journey.

And really, every change we go through is simultaneously a beginning and an ending of something in *some* way, so I think we should let ourselves fall in love with all of it... including with the unknown, and with the planting of the seeds, and with all of the butterflies and adrenaline highs that we get to feel during the unfolding of things.

some people are just light, glow,
hope… human stars.

keep your way
of being love, keep this glow,
others will come to you
just to feel this

the sunkissed ones,
they leave a sweetness with you
that changes the
air you breathe forever

if they love you,
they will love the way
you fall in love with yourself,
and life, and them,
and everything beautiful

i love in flowers, soft
i love in fire, wild
i love in sky, free
i love in stars, forever

i love in energy

how her eyes dream
how her lips say heaven
how that heart holds a universe
and that sweet in her smile means...

let go and run wild with me

we have
wilderness hearts,
we get restless with the moon,
we're meant to live in wild opens,
and run free under
starlight

we crave
a *soul-stirring*
love
and we
chase that
soul-stirring
life

let me
wander with
the ones who are
tangled in stars
and tethered
to promise

- *dreamers*

just take me somewhere that
takes my breath away

Directions...

a southern girl
with a gypsy soul, she took
a journey west to help her grow,
and then she chased the eastern sun
to give her faith,
and she let the northern lights
guide her way
...home.

i like you brave,

i like you breathing free,

i like you feeling all of you in you

you have a breathtaking wildfire heart

let your head quiet,
go where your heart sways

paper planes,
or angel wings, anything
to lift the heavy, to let her dream...

she's always been searching for some
way to escape gravity

how

you look for

magic

unfailingly,

that's your treasure,

that's your gold

shy...
but *curious*

just because
benevolence
and butterflies
linger on your tongue,
it does not mean
your voice cannot be
a revolution

- *soft-spoken girls*

she's made up
of sweet tea and poetry

- *country girl*

stay in
your sweetness,
don't let anything take
that from you

present.
patient.
peaceful.

to be steady in the soul
and free in the spirit

steady and free

may the
sunrise bring you peace
and fill your soul with
possibility

there's something
about the way dawn whispers
"so much is out there waiting"
that keeps my dreams breathing...

there's just a way
that morning carries hope.

i've been letting go
of heavy things

and i've been healing
a spirit, and tending to a soul, and
listening to a heart. and i've started to
exhale. and to breathe in... and to
breathe. in. *a life*

...and i've been letting go of
so, *so many* heavy things

let it all be light,
and new, and undiscovered

beautiful
wildflower...
be free and reach
for the sun,
live in all your colors
and grow so
untamed

go where you breathe free

like a butterfly,
her wings unfolded

she's flowers and fire

'she's flowers and fire'
is the second poetry collection by butterflies rising.
It is another book of poetry written in her sensitive and vulnerable style but has a different, fiery energy to it.
It also includes more in-depth personal meaning behind the poems and more of the longer prose poems.
Available on Amazon | shesflowersandfire.com/book

go where you breathe free

'go where you breathe free'
is an inspiration writing journal by butterflies rising that is inspired by her poem 'just go (go where you breathe free).' It has blank and full-color decorative pages for journaling and includes butterflies rising quotes and poems throughout. It's perfect for a writing journal or a travel journal and hopes to provide some inspiration for your spirit.
Available on Amazon | gowhereyoubreathefree.com/book

$5.00 postcard size prints

4 x 6 postcard size prints with butterflies rising poems and quotes in the butterflies rising poetry shop: butterfliesrisingpoetry.com

Made in the USA
Las Vegas, NV
12 July 2022